Write it in Arabic

A Workbook and Step-by-Step
Guide to Writing the Arabic Alphabet

Naglaa Ghali

Second Edition

Fun with Arabic

Requests for permission to make copies of any part of the work should be e-mailed to Fun with Arabic, info@funwitharabic.com

Library and Archives Canada Cataloguing in Publication

Ghali, Naglaa
        Write it in Arabic : a workbook and step-by-step guide to writing the Arabic alphabet / Naglaa Ghali. — 2nd ed.

ISBN 978-0-9730512-3-0

        1. Arabic alphabet. 2. Arabic language—Writing. 3. Arabic language—Vocabulary. 4. Arabic language—Problems, exercises, etc. 5. Arabic language—Textbooks for second language learners—English speakers. I. Title.

PJ6123.G43 2009   492.781'3   C2008-906422-4

This book was printed in China.

    2 3 4 5   13 12 11

All inquiries should be addressed to
info@funwitharabic.com
http://www.funwitharabic.com

Contents

Unit 2: Variants and Vowels

Part Two

Preface

Write it in Arabic is an alphabet guide and workbook that offers a hands-on approach to learning Arabic. Away from lengthy introductions and linguistic complications, this book will lead you directly into unravelling the mystery of the Arabic script and learning how to read and write it.

In this book, you will be introduced to the Arabic alphabet in sequence. You will practice writing the shape of each letter and you will learn how to join the letters to form words. This book will also guide you in the pronunciation of the different letters of the alphabet. You should become familiar with the shape and sound of each letter before moving on to the next one.

The words provided in the exercises have been carefully selected to help you practice the letters that you have already learned, while enriching your vocabulary. A set of easy-to-follow exercises is also included in Part Two. These exercises are designed to help you practice the Arabic style of writing and teach you new, frequently used, Arabic words.

By the end of the workbook, you should have a strong grasp of the Arabic alphabet and knowledge of its shape and sound. This will assist you greatly in further Arabic studies.

The Arabic Language

Arabic is spoken by more than 250 million people in over 22 countries. It is the official language of all Arab countries, hence forming a cultural bond among them. Arabic belongs to the Semitic group of languages which includes Hebrew, Aramaic, Ethiopic and others.

There are three basic forms of the language: classical, modern, and colloquial. The classical form is the language of old literary Arabic and the Arabic of the Qu'ran. The Modern Standard Arabic (MSA) form is the written and official language of the Arab world today. The colloquial form is the commonly spoken Arabic, which differs greatly from one country to another. Written Arabic, however, remains the same throughout the Arab world. The Arabic alphabet has also been adopted, with some modifications, by non-Semitic languages, including Persian, Urdu, Malay, and Pashto.

This workbook will introduce you to Modern Standard Arabic, which is the written language of the Arab world today. Although this form is not the commonly spoken language, it is widely understood in all Arab countries, and shares several similarities with classical Arabic. You might sound out of place if you try to converse in Modern Standard Arabic, since the colloquial form is usually spoken. Nevertheless, this is the proper form of the language. The purpose of this book is to provide you with the basic skills for reading, writing, and understanding Arabic as it appears in newspapers, current literature, and educational materials.

1

Before You Start

The Arabic alphabet consists of 28 letters. The letters are written from right to left. To remain faithful to Arabic written work, this book opens like any book printed in Arabic. As well, you will write from right to left when completing the exercises.

When you write in Arabic, you join the letters together to form words. The shape of most letters changes according to their position in a word. There are, however, six letters that never change shape. In this book, we will refer to them as "disjoined letters." These letters do not join the letters following them and their shape does not change according to their position in a word. Joined letters, on the other hand, join the letters on their left and right. Most joined letters have more than one form. The short form of the letter is used at the beginning of a word or when it falls between two other joined letters. The long form is used when the letter falls at the end of a word or when it stands alone.

To complete the exercises in this workbook, start at the dot and follow the arrows. Try your best not to lift your pen when writing. Start with the basic shape of the letter, and then place any additional dots or strokes. Remember, any additional marks are placed from right to left. Pay attention to the writing line, and note which parts of the letter belong above or beneath the line. Do not confuse the name of the letter with its pronunciation. In Arabic, the name of the letter does not necessarily correspond to the sound it produces.

3

Part One

Letters and Numbers

alif

alif

The *alif* is the first letter of the Arabic alphabet. It is a disjoined letter. This means that it does not join the letter following it. It does, however, join the letter preceding it, that is, the letter to its right. The *alif* is written as a vertical stroke from top to bottom. It has only one form and it rests on the writing line.

When the *alif* is joined to its right, it is written as a vertical stroke from the bottom up. The *alif* represents the long vowel *aa*. It can also represent the short vowels *a, i,* or *u,* which depends on its vocalisation (see pages 48 and 54).

7

baa', taa', and thaa'

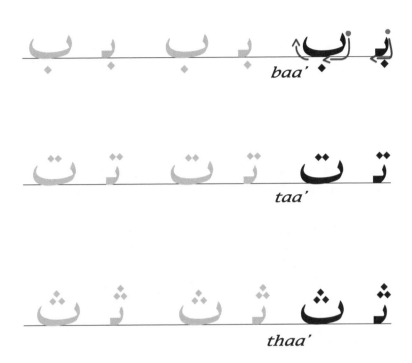

baa'

taa'

thaa'

The *baa'*, *taa',* and *thaa'* are all joined letters and each has two forms. The short form of the letter is used at the beginning of a word or between two other joined letters. The full form is written when the letter falls at the end of a word or when it stands alone.

The dot under the *baa'* is an integral part of the letter and must not be omitted. Similarly, the two dots on the *taa'* and the three dots on the *thaa'* must be kept.

8

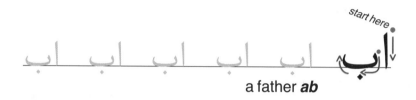

a father *ab*

door *baab*

daddy *baabaa*

to broadcast *bathth*

steadiness *thabaat*

9

geem, Haa', and khaa'

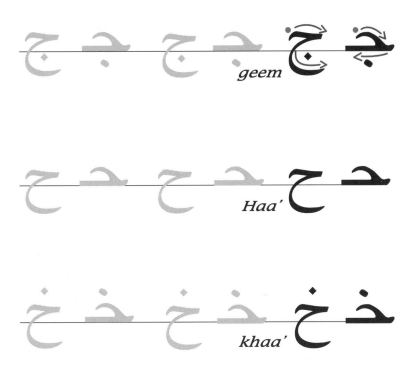

geem

Haa'

khaa'

These three letters belong to the category of joined letters. They each have a short and long form and their shape changes according to their position in a word. The *geem* (also known as jiim) has a dot underneath, the *Haa'* has no dots, and the *khaa'* has one dot on top.

The short form rests on the writing line. The full form starts above the line and then curls beneath it.

حب حب حب حب حب حب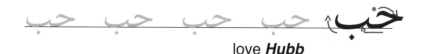

love *Hubb*

اخت اخت اخت اخت اخت اخت

sister *ukht*

بحث بحث بحث بحث بحث بحث

research *baHth*

باح باح باح باح باح باح

to reveal *baaH*

تحت تحت تحت تحت تحت تحت

under/below *taHt*

Notes and Review:
First Set of Letters

☾ The letters *baa'* (ب), *taa'* (ت) and *thaa'* (ث)
are easy to pronounce. The *baa'* is similar to the
English letter *b*, as in the word "boy." Note that in
the Arabic language there is no equivalent to the
letter *p*, so the *baa'* is always used to transliterate
the *p*.

☾ The *taa'* has a familiar sound, much like the English
letter *t* as in "toy."

☾ The *thaa'* has no direct equivalent in English. Its
sound is similar to the letters *th* as in "theatre."

☾ The *geem* (ج) has two possible pronunciations,
which depend on the specific dialect used. In
Egyptian Arabic, for example, it is pronounced *g* as
in "gap." Most other dialects pronounce it more like
a *j* as in "John."

☾ The *Haa'* (ح) is difficult to learn because it has no
direct equivalent in English. The closest sound is
the English letter *h*. The *Haa',* however, has a more
emphatic and heavy sound than the *h* (see page
42). When we refer to the *Haa',* we will capitalise it
to indicate the emphatic sound it produces.

☾ The *khaa'* (خ) sounds like the letters *kh* as in
"Khan" or *ch* as in "Bach."

12

to urge/incite **Haththa**

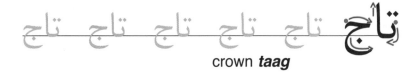

crown **taag**

pilgrimage **Hagg**

luck **bakht**

researcher **baaHith**

daal and dhaal

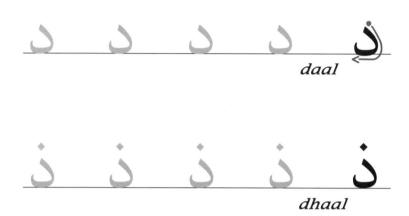

daal

dhaal

The *daal* and *dhaal* are both disjoined letters. They do not join the letter that follows, and their shape does not change according to their position in a word. They have only one form each, and they both rest on the writing line. The *dhaal* has one dot on top, while the *daal* has none.

The *daal* is equivalent to the English letter *d* as in "dad." The *dhaal* has no direct equivalent in English. The closest sound is the letters *th* as in "this" or as in "with." The *dhaal* is usually transliterated as *dh*.

14

دب دب دب دب دب دب دب دب

a bear *dubb*

جد جد جد جد جد جد جد

grandfather *gadd*

بجد بجد بجد بجد بجد بجد

seriously *bigad*

جذب جذب جذب جذب جذب

to attract *gadhdhaba*

ذباب ذباب ذباب ذباب ذباب

flies (insect) *dhubaab*

raa' and zaay

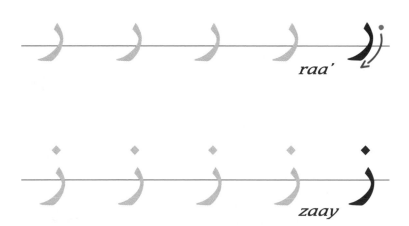

raa'

zaay

The *raa'* and *zaay* (also known as *zayn*) belong to the family of disjoined letters and have only one form each. Both letters share the same basic shape. The *zaay*, however, has a dot on top while the *raa'* has none. Each letter starts above the writing line and then curves below it. Note that approximately one third of the letter appears above the line and two thirds beneath it.

The sound of the letter *raa'* is similar to the English letter *r* as in "Rome." The *zaay* is equivalent to the letter *z* as is "zoo."

16

rice *aruzz*

war *Harb*

cold *bard*

neighbour *gaar*

glass *zugaag*

17

seen and sheen

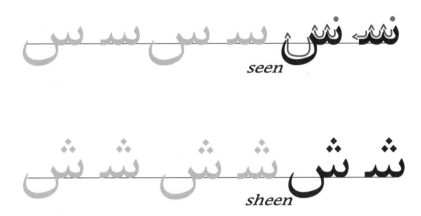

seen

sheen

The *seen* and *sheen* belong to the family of joined letters. They each have a short and a long form. The two letters share the same shape except that the *sheen* has three dots arranged as a triangle on top.

The short form rests on the writing line. The long form starts on the line and then descends underneath it, forming a semicircle.

The letter *seen* is equivalent to the English letter *s*. The *sheen* sounds like the letters *sh* as in "she."

18

mister/professor **ustaadh**

bell **garas**

foundation **asaas**

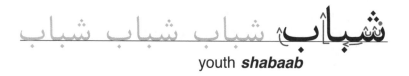

youth **shabaab**

to scratch **khadasha**

Saad and Daad

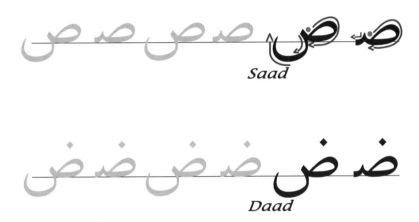

Saad

Daad

These two letters have no direct equivalent in English. *The Saad* sounds like a heavy *s.* Try pronouncing the word "sun" while stressing the *s.* The *Daad* also has no equivalent in English. The closest pronunciation to the letter *Daad* is the sound of a stressed *d* as in the English word "dome."

Both letters belong to the family of joined letters and they have two forms each. The short form of the letter rests on the writing line. The long form starts on the line, curves underneath it, and then comes up again to rest just above the line. Take special note of the upward stroke in the short form of both letters.

morning **SabaaH**

خصد حصد حصد حصد

to harvest **HaSada**

خاص خاص خاص خاص

private **khaaSS**

ضبازب ضباب ضباب ضباب

fog **Dabaab**

land **arD**

Taa' and Zaa'

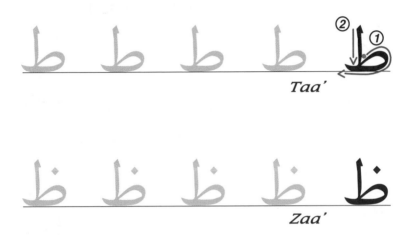

Taa'

Zaa'

Taa' and *Zaa'* belong to the family of joined letters. However, they have only one form each and their shape does not change according to their position in a word. They rest on the writing line. To write the letters, start with the bottom part first and add the stroke. Then, add a dot on the Zaa'

Neither of these letters has a direct equivalent in English. The *Taa'* sounds like a bold or stressed *t*. The *Zaa'* (which has one dot) sounds like a stressed *z*.

cook **Tabbaakh**

mistake/error **khaTa'**

duck **baTT**

luck **HaZZ**

officer **DaabiT**

Notes and Review:
Second Set of Letters

You have been introduced to four new letters whose sounds are unfamiliar to non-Arabic speakers: *Saad* (ص), *Daad* (ض), *Taa'* (ط), and *Zaa'* (ظ). However, they are not hard to master. These letters do have familiar equivalents in English, but they need to be pronounced much more forcefully and in a deeper tone. In this book, we will capitalise all references to these letters to indicate the emphatic sound they produce.

Pay careful attention that you distinguish the sounds of these letters from similar letters learned previously. The similar couples are as follows:

℃ The *Saad* (ص) and the *seen* (س): The *seen* sounds like the English letter *s*, while the *Saad* sounds like a deep and bold *s*

℃ The *Daad* (ض) and the *daal* (د): The *daal* is equivalent to the English letter *d*, while the *Daad* is a more forceful and bolder *d*.

℃ The *Taa'* (ط) and the *taa'* (ت): The letter *Taa'* is a bold strong *t*. The letter *taa'* is the direct equivalent to the letter *t*.

℃ Finally, do not mistake the sound of the *Zaa'* (ظ) for the *zaay* (ز). The *Zaa'* is a strong bold *z*, while the *zaay* is the direct equivalent to the English letter *z*.

24

patience **Sabr**

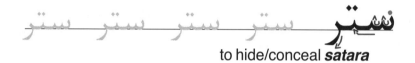

to hide/conceal ***satara***

line ***saTr***

lesson ***dars***

tooth ***Dirs***

ʿayn

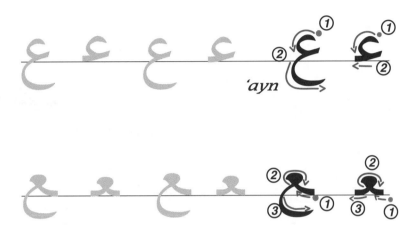

The *ʿayn* is difficult to learn. It is a joined letter and has four different shapes. The first, reading from right to left, appears at the beginning of a word and rests on the writing line.

The second shape is used when the *ʿayn* is standing alone, or at the end of a word after a disjoined letter. It begins just above the line and continues underneath.

The third form of the *ʿayn* falls in the middle of a word between two joined letters. The last example, shows the *ʿayn* when it falls at the end of a word after a joined letter. It begins on top of the line and then curves below it.

perfume *ᶜiTr*

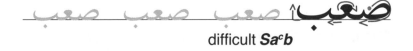

street *shaariᶜ*

difficult *Saᶜb*

of course *Tabᶜan*

quarter *rubᶜ*

ghayn

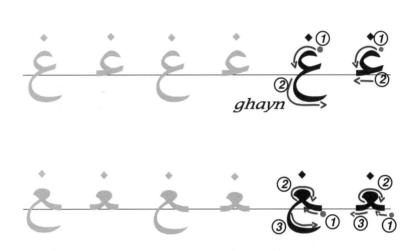

The *ghayn* is similar in shape to the letter *'ayn*; the only difference is that the *ghayn* has a dot on top while the *'ayn* has none.

The *'ayn* and *ghayn* have no direct equivalent in English. Their sounds are not familiar to most non-Arabic speakers. You need to listen carefully to their pronunciation and try to practice the sound. The *ghayn* is transliterated as *gh*, while the *'ayn* is usually transcribed as *ᶜ* indicating that this sound is unique and there is no match in the English alphabet. If you still find it hard to master the sound of the *'ayn*, try to think of it as an emphatic or long *a*, as in Verdi's opera "Aida." This is not really accurate, but it will be the closest sound it imitates. The closest sound for the *ghayn* are the letters *gh* in "Baghdad."

28

raven **ghuraab**

west **gharb**

tomorrow **ghadan**

Baghdad

tobacco **tibgh**

29

faa' and qaaf

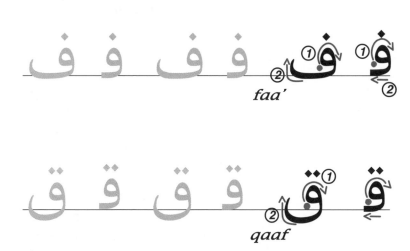

faa'

qaaf

The *faa'* and *qaaf* share the same short form, but their long forms are different. Their short forms rest on the writing line. The *faa'* has one dot while the *qaaf* has two. The long form of the *faa'* is elongated and rests on the line, whereas that of the *qaaf* starts just above the line and then descends beneath it forming half a circle.

Faa' is similar to the English letter *f*. The *qaaf* has no direct equivalent; the closest you can find to its sound is the letter *q* as in "Iraq."

فقد فقد فقد فقد فقد **فقد**

to lose *faqada*

تفاح تفاح تفاح تفاح تفاح **تفاح**

apples *tuffaaH*

قطف قطف قطف قطف **قطف**

to pick (e.g. flowers) *qaTafa*

قطار قطار قطار قطار **قطار**

train *qiTaar*

شرق شرق شرق شرق شرق **شرق**

east *sharq*

kaaf

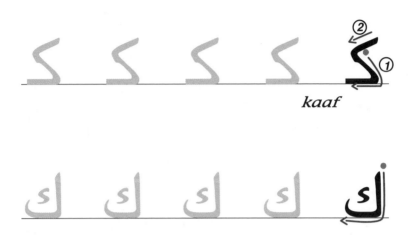

kaaf

Kaaf is a joined letter, and has two forms. The short form is used in the beginning or middle of a word. To write the *kaaf,* start with the base of the letter and then add the top stroke.

The full form occurs when the letter stands alone or at the end of a word. The full form rests on the writing line. What's inside the *kaaf* is a *hamza,* (see page 48). It is an integral part of the letter, but has no effect on its pronunciation.

The letter *kaaf* is similar in its pronunciation to the English letter *k*.

book *kitaab*

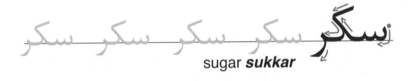

sugar *sukkar*

thank you *shukran*

كَشك

kiosk *kushk*

شباك

window *shubbaak*

33

laam

laam

The *laam* is similar to the English letter *l*. It is a joined letter and has two forms. The short form rests on the writing line. The full form starts above the line; its tail descends below the line and then curves up again just above it.

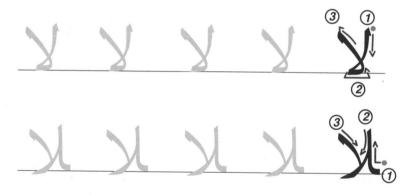

The *laam* and the *alif* have a unique shape when they are joined together. The first example shows the two letters when standing alone. The second shape is used when the *laam* is joined from its right; it then connects with the *alif* to form this distinctive shape. Remember that the *alif* is a disjoined letter, meaning it never joins the letter following it.

34

liter *litr*

كلب

dog *kalb*

الف

thousand *alf*

فلفل

pepper *filfil*

hills *tilaal*

Notes and Review:

The Prefix *alif laam*

At this point, let us pause to discuss the definite article "the."

In Arabic there is no equivalent to the English "the." The prefix *alif laam* (ﺍﻟ) serves instead as the definite article. It is also worth noting that in Arabic an adjective has to agree with a noun; if the noun is masculine or feminine, definite or indefinite, singular or plural, the adjective must follow the same form.

In the last two examples (on the facing page) you will notice that since the *alif laam* prefix indicates that the noun is definite, its adjective must have the prefix agree as well.

You will find the definite article used more frequently in Arabic than in English, especially in general terms and in expressions like love, life, or patience. For example, "life is beautiful" becomes "the life is beautiful."

There are no indefinite articles such as "a" and "an" in the Arabic language, you simply leave them out.

36

الصبر

patience ***al-Sabr***

الرجل

the man ***al-ragul***

الاخبار

the news ***al-akhbaar***

الدور الرابع

the fourth floor ***al-dawr al-raabiᶜ***

البرد القارس

the bitter cold ***al-bard al-qaaris***

meem

meem

The letter *meem* corresponds to the English letter *m* as in "moon." It is a joined letter with two forms. The short form rests on the writing line, while the full form begins on the line and then descends underneath it.

When the final *meem* is joined to another letter, it is usually written as a circle counter-clockwise. After completing the circle, you add the tail.

38

king *malik*

airport *maTaar*

moon *qamar*

complete/perfect *tamaam*

restaurant *maTᶜam*

noon

noon

The *noon* is a joined letter with two forms. The short form rests on the writing line and is similar in shape to the letters *baa'* (ب), *taa'* (ت), and *thaa'* (ث), which you studied earlier. The long form is different. It is round, resembling half a circle, and begins above the line and then curls underneath it.

The *noon* has only one dot, positioned as shown above. The dot is an integral part of the letter. Remember, it is always best to write the basic part of the letter first, and then add any additional dots or strokes. The *noon* is similar in its pronunciation to the English letter *n* as in "near."

fire **naar**

bank **bank**

milk **laban**

tenderness **Hanaan**

فنجان

cup **fingaan**

41

haa'

haa'

The *haa'* has four shapes. Reading from right to left, you notice the first form, when the *haa'* falls at the beginning of a word. The second form—the egg-shaped *haa'*—illustrates the letter when standing alone or at the end of a word after a disjoined letter. The third form occurs when the *haa'* falls between two joined letters, and the last shape, when the *haa'* falls at the end of a word after a joined letter.

The *haa'* is pronounced like the English letter *h*. Many students of the Arabic language confuse the sounds of the *haa'* and the *Haa'* (ح). The latter (see page 10) has no equivalent in English, but sounds like a heavily accented *h*.

42

pyramid **haram**

hoopoe (type of bird) **hudhud**

attention **intibaah**

month **shahr**

pound (currency) **gineeh**

43

waaw

waaw

The *waaw* is similar in pronunciation to the English letter *w*. It can also represent the long vowel *oo*. The letter starts with a circle written clockwise, which starts and ends on the line. The tail of the letter descends in a slight curve beneath the writing line. The *waaw* is another disjoined letter and has only one form.

Remember, a disjoined letter joins the letter to its right, but **does not join** the letter that follows it. Disjoined letters have only one shape, as their form does not change according to their position in a word. The six disjoined letters are the *alif* (١), *daal* (د), *dhaal* (ذ), *raa'* (ر), *zaay* (ز), and *waaw* (و).

ورق

paper *waraq*

لون

colour *lawn*

صوت

voice/sound *Sawt*

ورد

flowers *ward*

وصول

arrival *wuSool*

45

yaa'

yaa'

The *yaa'* has two forms. The short form should by now look familiar to you. This time it rests on the writing line with two dots underneath. The full form is unique. It starts above the line, curves beneath it, and then up again. The two dots underneath the full form are sometimes ignored (see page 52). Remember, the short form of the letter is used at the beginning of a word, or when it falls between two other joined letters. The full form appears when the letter is standing alone or at the end of a word.

The *yaa'* is similar to the English letter *y*. It can also represent the sound of the long vowel *ee*.

day **yawm**

right **yameen**

tea **shaay**

taxi **taaksee**

my love **Habeebee**

hamza

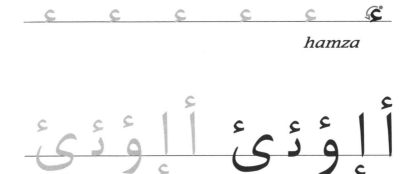

hamza

The *hamza* has no specific sound. It indicates a glottal stop. It is usually transcribed as an apostrophe and it indicates a vocal break. The *hamza* is usually carried by the *alif*, the *waaw*, or the *yaa'*. It can also occur alone at the end of a word; in this case the *hamza* is placed on the writing line.

The *hamza* and the *alif* have a unique relationship together. The *hamza* can occur above or under the *alif*. When the *hamza* occurs above the letter, (أ) the *alif* is pronounced as an *a*. When the *hamza* occurs underneath, the *alif* (إ) is pronounced as an *i*.

news *anbaa'*

dictation *imlaa'*

question *su'aal*

president *ra'ees*

thing *shee'*

49

taa' marbooTa

taa' marbooTa

The *taa' marbooTa* is not an alphabet letter; it is more of a feminine mark. In Arabic, all nouns are either masculine or feminine. Most, although not all, feminine nouns end with the *taa' marbooTa*. A masculine noun can end in any letter. Remember that a noun and an adjective have to agree, so if a noun is feminine, its adjective will also end with the same feminine mark.

For example:

Happy family	*ᶜaa'ila saᶜeeda*	عائلة سعيدة
Pretty woman	*imra'a gameela*	امرأة جميلة

The *taa' marbooTa* is found only at the end of a word. It has two forms that are a variation of the letter *haa'* (see page 42). The egg shape with two dots is used when the *taa' marbooTa* falls at the end of a word after a disjoined letter. The second shape is used when it falls at the end of a word after a joined letter. The *taa' marbooTa* is commonly pronounced as an *a*.

دكتور دكتور دكتور دكتور **دكتور**

doctor *duktoor*

دكتورة دكتورة دكتورة دكتورة **دكتورة**

doctor (female) *duktoora*

جميلة جميلة جميلة جميلة **جميلة**

pretty *gameela*

قهوة قهوة قهوة قهوة قهوة **قهوة**

coffee *qahwa*

هدية هدية هدية هدية **هدية**

gift *hadeeya*

51

alif maqSoora

The *alif maqSoora* looks like the final letter *yaa'* with no dots underneath (see page 46). The *alif maqSoora* can only fall in the end of a word. It is pronounced as a long vowel "aa."

The *alif maqSoora* can be confusing to a new learner. Often the final *yaa'* (which represents the y or the long vowel "ee") is written as a ى with no dots underneath. This can be considered as an element of style. In Egyptian Arabic, for example, both the *yaa'* and *alif maqSoora* are written as ى.

Remember, then, that a final ى can represent an *alif maqSoora* pronounced as "aa" or it can represent the letter *yaa'* pronounced as a "y" or "ee."

شَكْوَى شكوى شكوى شكوى شكوى

complaint *shakwaa*

سَلْمَى سلمى سلمى سلمى سلمى

Salmaa (the proper name)

مَرْمَى مرمى مرمى مرمى

goal *marmaa*

ذِكْرَى ذكرى ذكرى ذكرى ذكرى

anniversary *dhikraa*

مُوسِيقَى موسيقى موسيقى موسيقى

music *mooseeqaa*

53

Vowel marks

Arabic has three special vowel marks, which are not letters of the alphabet.

The *kasra* (‿).

The *kasra* looks like a small diagonal stroke. It is written below the consonant it vocalises and represents the short vowel *i* as in "pit."

The *fatHaa* (´)

The *fatHaa* looks exactly like the *kasra*. It is written above the letter and represents the vowel *a* as in "sat".

The *Damma* (ُ)

The *Damma* looks like a small *waaw*. It is written above the letter and represents the short vowel *u* as in "put."

Example:

baa' and a *kasra*   بِ is pronounced bi

baa' and *fatHaa*   بَ is pronounced ba

baa' and a *Damma*   بُ is pronounced bu

The pronunciation of a word, and therefore its meaning, can change according to its vocalisation. This is demonstrated in the examples on the facing page.

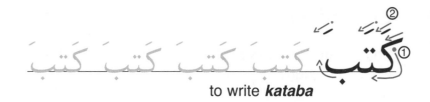

to write *kataba*

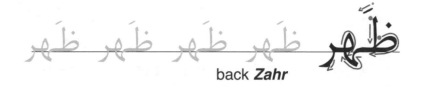

books *kutub*

back *Zahr*

to appear *Zahara*

noon *Zuhr*

Other Signs

Some marks are not vowels, but they do affect the way a word is pronounced.

shadda (ّ)

In Arabic, if a word has a double letter, the letter is not written twice. Rather, this is indicated by a *shadda* (ّ) above the consonant. The *shadda* looks like a small *seen* and is written on top of the letter. When the *shadda* occurs above a consonant, that consonant is pronounced as a double letter.

to stop **kaffa**

In the above example, the *shadda* on top of the *faa'* indicates that this is a double letter.

tanween (ً)

The *tanween* mark resembles two *fatHas* stacked on top of each other (ً). The *tanween* sounds like an *n* and usually appears over the *alif*. It can only occur at the end of a word.

thank you **shukran**

madda (˜)

The *madda* is placed above the *alif*. It usually falls at the beginning of the word. Its presence indicates a stretched *alif* or a long vowel "aa".

miss ***aanisa***

sukoon (o)

The *sukoon* looks like a little circle. It is the vowelesness mark. If it occurs above a consonant, it indicates that this consonant cannot be followed by a vowel.

yes ***na^cam***

Look at this word and notice that both the *noon and the 'ayn* carry the short vowel "a." The *meem*, however, is not followed by any vowels. This is indicated by the *sukoon* mark. This sign is rarely written in Modern Standard Arabic.

Remember, when writing Arabic, start by writing the basic shape of the letter, then add any strokes or dots, and then place any vocalisation marks.

57

school *madrasa*

teacher (female) *mudarrisa*

similar *mithl*

to perform/to act *maththala*

مَثَل

proverb *mathal*

كَمْ   كَمْ   كَمْ   كَمْ   كَمْ   كَمْ

how many **kam**

بين   بين   بين   بين   بين   بين

between **bayna**

مِرآة   مِرآة   مِرآة   مِرآة   مِرآة   مِرآة

mirror **mir'aah**

آسِف   آسِف   آسِف   آسِف   آسِف   آسِف

sorry **aasif**

الآن   الآن   الآن   الآن   الآن

now **al'aan**

immediately *fawran*

very *giddan*

hello/welcome *ahlan*

welcome *marHaban*

pardon ᶜ*afwan*

significant *haamm*

apartment *shaqqa*

story *qiSSa*

hot *Haarr*

freedom *Hurreeya*

Numbers

The number system we use in English was developed from the Arabic more than 500 years ago, and is today commonly known as the Arabic numeral system. Over the years, however, numbers in both parts of the world evolved in different ways. For our purposes, we will refer to numbers used in English as "European numerals" and those used in the Arabic language as "Arabic numerals."

As both systems share the same origin, there are a number of similarities between Arabic and European numerals. Most importantly, numbers composed in Arabic are written from left to right, exactly as in English. So, when you combine words and numbers, you read the word from right to left, but the number from left to right.

Example: **House No. 6702**

Translates to: بيت رقم : ٦٧٠٢

☪ Pay careful attention to the zero (◆), which resembles a dot, and the five (٥), which resembles a zero in European numerals.

☪ In North African countries, European numerals are used in place of Arabic ones, which means that the previous example reads: **6702** :بيت رقم

☪ Today, with new Web technologies, you will find many Arabic Web sites using European numerals instead of Arabic ones.

١ ٢ ٣   ١ ٢ ٣   ١ ٢ ٣   ١ ٢ ٣

                                             3   2   1

٤ ٥ ٦   ٤ ٥ ٦   ٤ ٥ ٦   ٤ ٥ ٦

                                             6   5   4

٧ ٨ ٩   ٧ ٨ ٩   ٧ ٨ ٩   ٧ ٨ ٩

                                           9   8   7

١٠ ١١ ١٢   ١٠ ١١ ١٢   ١٠ ١١ ١٢

                                        12 11 10

٢٠ ٢١ ٢٢   ٢٠ ٢١ ٢٢   ٢٠ ٢١ ٢٢

                                        22 21 20

٣٠ ٤٠ ٥٠   ٣٠ ٤٠ ٥٠   ٣٠ ٤٠ ٥٠

                                        50 40 30

63

٦٥   ٦٥   ٦٥   ٦٥   ٦٥   **٦٥**

65

١٧٠   ١٧٠   ١٧٠   ١٧٠   ١٧٠   **١٧٠**

170

٦٨٠٣   ٦٨٠٣   ٦٨٠٣   **٦٨٠٣**

6803

٢٤٥٦٨   ٢٤٥٦٨   **٢٤٥٦٨**

24568

٣٩١٠٦٤٥٧   **٣٩١٠٦٤٥٧**

39106457

الساعة ١٢ الساعة ١٢ الساعة ١٢

12 o'clock   *al-saaᶜa ithnaashar*

٤٥٠ مدعو ٤٥٠ مدعو ٤٥٠ مدعو

450 guests   *rubᶜumya wa-khamseen madᶜoo*

شارع٣٠٨ شارع٣٠٨ شارع٣٠٨

street 308   *shaariᶜ thulthumeea wa-thamaaniya*

١٦٠ دولار ١٦٠ دولار ١٦٠ دولار

160 dollars   *mi'a wa-sitteen doolaar*

صفحة ٧٩ صفحة ٧٩ صفحة ٧٩

page 79   *safHaa tisᶜa wa-sabᶜeen*

65

Handwriting

ح حد جج ثث تت بب ا

ش شــ ســـ ز ر ذ د خخ

غغ عع ظ ط ضض صص

ن نن م مه لل كك قق فف

يي يـ و ه هـ

١ ٢ ٢ ٣ ٤ ٥ ٦ ٧ ٨ ٩ ٠١

Until now, we have concentrated on the printed version of the Arabic alphabet. There are only a few differences between printed and handwritten Arabic. The next few pages will guide you through handwritten script. It is recommended, however, that you learn the classic or printed form of writing first, since you can't go wrong with printing. As your comfort level with the alphabet progresses, you will be able to develop your own writing style.

Notes on Handwriting

ⓒ When a letter has more than one dot on top or bottom, the dots are usually joined together. For example, the two dots under the *yaa'* (ـﻱ) join to form a dash, and the three dots on top of the *thaa'* (ـﺙ) form a triangle.

ⓒ In handwritten Arabic, the *seen* (ـﺱ) and the *sheen* (ـﺵ) lose their sharp upward points and are written as a flat line.

ⓒ Letters that end with a dot, such as the *noon, Daad, qaaf,* and *sheen,* are sometimes written with an outside stroke in place of the dot (ﻕ ﺽ ﺵ ﻥ).

ⓒ The final *noon* can be written in two different ways. The dot can be replaced by an outside stroke or it can coil inside the letter (ﻥ ﻥ).

ⓒ When writing the *kaaf*, a curl can sometimes be placed inside it, instead of the *hamza* (ﻙ).

ⓒ The middle *haa'* is handwritten as (ﺣ) and the final form can be written as: ﺢ. Similarly, the *taa' marbooTa* will be written as: ﺔ.

ⓒ In numbers, the upward point of number two is flattened out (٢), and number three (٣) loses one of its points. Note that the number three in handwriting resembles the number two in print; try not to confuse them.

67

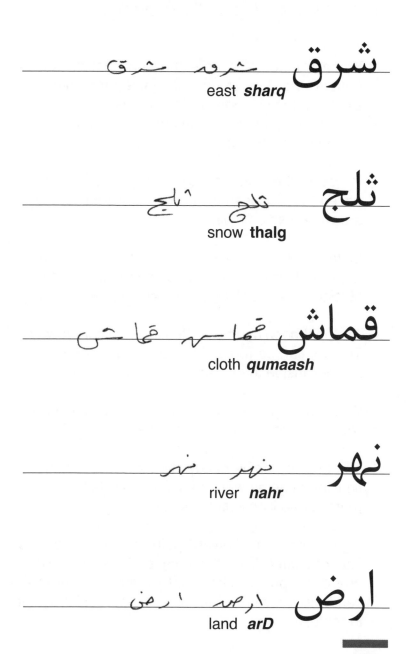

شرق
east **sharq**

ثلج
snow **thalg**

قماش
cloth **qumaash**

نهر
river **nahr**

ارض
land **arD**

مستشفى

hospital ***mustashfaa***

مشكلة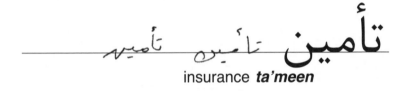

problem ***mushkila***

تأمين

insurance ***ta'meen***

جمرك

customs ***gumruk***

فندق

hotel ***funduq***

Part Two

Exercises

Exercise 1

In this exercise, you are given the short form of the letter. Write the long form. The first one has been done for you. Be sure to practice a few times.

ت ت ت ت ت -A

ح -F

ق -B

ش -G

ع -C

ا -H

ك -D

ف -I

م -E

ء -J

Exercise 2

In this exercise, you are given the long form of the letter. Write the short form. Practice a few times.

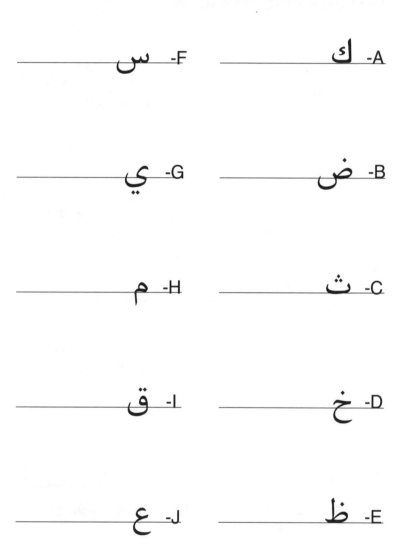

ك A-

_____

ض B-

_____

ث C-

_____

خ D-

_____

ظ E-

_____

س F-

_____

ي G-

_____

م H-

_____

ق I-

_____

ع J-

_____

Exercise 3

Write the missing letters in the squares provided. The first exercise is done for you.

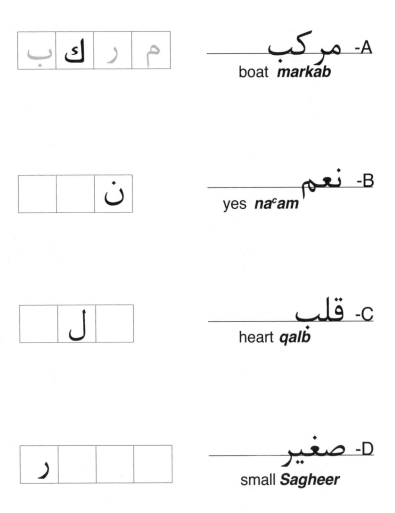

A- مركب
boat **markab**

B- نعم
yes **naᶜam**

C- قلب
heart **qalb**

D- صغير
small **Sagheer**

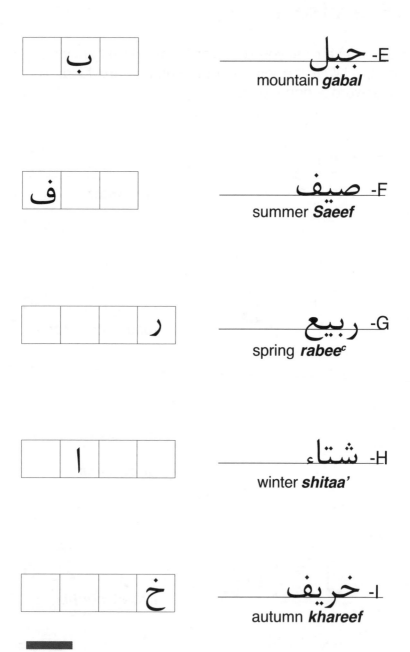

E-جبل _____
mountain *gabal*

F-صيف _____
summer *Saeef*

G-ربيع _____
spring *rabee*

H-شتاء _____
winter *shitaa'*

I-خريف _____
autumn *khareef*

Exercise 4

In this exercise, you are given the words in handwritten script. Write the letters in the squares provided. The first word is done for you.

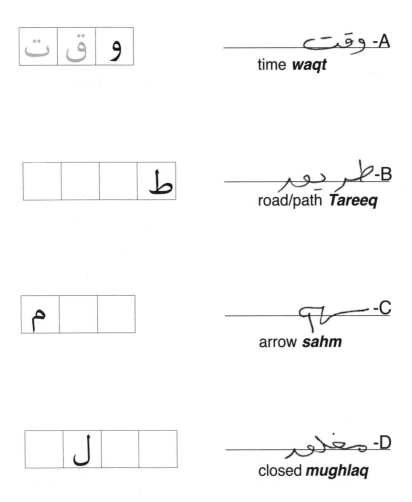

و	ق	ت

A- وقت

time **waqt**

			ط

B- طريق

road/path **Tareeq**

م		

C- سهم

arrow **sahm**

	ل		

D- مغلق

closed **mughlaq**

E- حــريّة

freedom **Hurreeya**

F- صـديـم

friend **Sadeeq**

G- خـروج

exit **khuroog**

H- سـلم

peace **salaam**

I- مفـتـش

inspector **mufattish**

Exercise 5

Match each profession to its Arabic equivalent. Use the transliteration as a guide. The first exercise is done for you.

i- Farmer
fallaaH

ii- Engineer
muhandis

iii- Journalist
SaHafee

iv- Teacher
mudarris

v- Lawyer
muHaamy

صحفي -A

فلّاح -B

محامي -C

مهندس -D

مدرّس -E

78

vi-Manager (female)
mudeera

سائق-F

vii- Driver
saa'iq

مديرة-G

viii-Consultant
mustashaar

صيدلي-H

ix- Employee (female)
muwaZZafa

ممرّضة-ا

x- Nurse (female)
mumarriDa

موظّفة-ل

xi- Pharmacist
Saydalee

مستشار-K

79

Exercise 6

Rearrange these Arab countries according to their alphabetical order.

F- ليبيا

Libya

A- مصر

Egypt

G- اليمن

Yemen

B- الاردن

Jordan

H- لبنان

Lebanon

C- سوريا

Syria

I- تونس

Tunisia

D- المغرب

Morocco

J- البحرين

Bahrain

E- قطر

Qatar

80

Exercise 7

Rearrange these Arab capitals according to their alphabetical order.

F- عمان _____ Amman

A- طرابلس _____ Tripoli

G- بغداد _____ Baghdad

B- الرياض _____ Riyadh

H- الرباط _____ Rabat

C- صنعاء _____ Sana'a

I- ابوظبي _____ Abu Dhabi

D- بيروت _____ Beirut

J- دمشق _____ Damascus

E- الخرطوم _____ Khartoum

Exercise 8

Match each Arabic number to its English equivalent.

i- 565   ١٢ -A

ii- 91   ١٩ -B

iii- 060   ٥٦٥ -C

iv- 19   ٩١ -D

v- 12   ٠٦٠ -E

Exercise 9

Match each of the following house and street numbers to its English equivalent.

i- House 985   A -شارع رقم ٨٥٠٦

ii- Street 6058   B -بيت رقم ٥٨٩

iii- Street 8056   C -شارع رقم ٨٠٥٦

iv- Street 8506   D -شارع رقم ٦٠٥٨

v- House 589   E -بيت رقم ٩٨٥

Exercise 10

Solve these simple equations. Remember, answers must be in Arabic.

$\underline{\hspace{3cm}} = ١٦ + ٢٤$ -F $\underline{\hspace{3cm}} = ٢٠ × ٤$ -A

$\underline{\hspace{3cm}} = ٧ ÷ ٢٨$ -G $\underline{\hspace{3cm}} = ١٠٠ - ٣٠٠$ -B

$\underline{\hspace{3cm}} = ٥٥ - ١٥٠$ -H $\underline{\hspace{3cm}} = ٤٥ + ٢٥$ -C

$\underline{\hspace{3cm}} = ٣ ÷ ٦٦$ -I $\underline{\hspace{3cm}} = ١٢ × ٨$ -D

$\underline{\hspace{3cm}} = ٥ × ٧$ -J $\underline{\hspace{3cm}} = ١٠ ÷ ٢٠$ -E

84

Exercise 11

Match each Arabic date, price, and quantity to its English equivalent.

i- 893/4 kilos   ٢٠٠٣/٧/١٨ -A

ii- 505 liras   ٥١٫٢٥ دولار -B

iii- 5.5 liras   ١٩٨١/٧/٣٠ -C

iv- 51.25 dollars   ٨٩٫٣/٤ كيلو -D

v- 25.51 dollars   ٥٠٥ ليرة -E

vi- 18/7/2003   ٥٫٥ ليرة -F

vii- 30/7/1981   ٢٥٫٥١ دولار -G

Exercise 12

Join the letters together to form a word. The first exercise is done for you.

A- ب ي ت بيت

house/home **bayt**

B- س و ق

market **sooq**

C- س ه م

arrow **sahm**

D- ن و ر

light **noor**

E- خ ط ر

danger **khaTar**

86

‎ع و ن م م‎ -F

forbidden **mamnoo**[c]

‎ة ع م ا ج‎ -G

university **gaamⁱa**

‎ر ي غ ص‎ -H

small **Sagheer**

‎ا ل ق ا ه ر ة‎ -I

Cairo **al-qaahira**

‎أ و ت و ب ي س‎ -J

bus **otobees**

K- ج ب ل
mountain *gabal*

L- ح ف ل ة
party *Hafla*

M- س ك و ت
silence *sukoot*

N- ص ح ر اء
desert *SaHraa'*

O- ص د ي ق
friend *Sadeeq*

P- ك ل ا م

talk *kalaam*

Q- ع ا ئ ل ة
family *ᶜaa'ila*

R- م غ ل ق
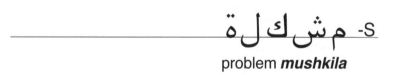
closed *mughlaq*

S- م ش ك ل ة
problem *mushkila*

T- ف ا ك ه ة

fruit *faakiha*

Exercise 13

Match each noun with an adjective. You are given the translation of the noun followed by the required adjective combination. However, of the three adjectives next to each noun, only one is correct.

A- يوم _____
Day (*good day*)

_____ سعيد
_____ سعيدة
_____ السعيد

B- البحر _____
Sea (*the far sea*)

_____ البعيدة
_____ بعيد
_____ البعيد

C- جبل _____
Mountain
(*a high mountain*)

_____ العالي
_____ عالي
_____ عالية

D- طفلة _____
Child (*naughty child*)

_____ شقية
_____ شقي
_____ الشقي

90

قديمة _____	_____ بيت -E
القديم _____	House
قديم _____	(an old house)

الجديد _____	_____ المديرة -F
جديدة _____	Manager
الجديدة _____	(the new manager)

النظيفة _____	_____ حجرة -G
نظيفة _____	Room
لانظيفة _____	(a clean room)

الثاني _____	_____ الدور -H
الثانية _____	Floor
ثاني _____	(the second floor)

Exercise 14

Make each adjective either definite or feminine according to the noun provided. The first example is done for you.

A- البحر (احمر)   البحر الاحمر

The Red Sea

B- المطعم (غالي)

_____

The expensive restaurant

C- الرجل (لطيف)

_____

The nice man

D- القهوة (ساخن)

_____

The hot coffee

E- امرأة (لطيف)

_____

A nice woman

92

F- الشارع (ضيق)

_____

The narrow street

G-الأخ (غني)

_____

The rich brother

H-الحجرة(مغلق)

_____

The closed room

ا- تذكرة(رخيص)

_____

A cheap ticket

ل-العصير(طازج)

_____

The fresh juice

K- الصديق(وفي)

_____

The loyal friend

Exercise 15

Match these words with the correct vocalisation. Use the transliteration as your guide.

i قَصة	
ii قُصّة	**A -قصة**
iii قصّة	story **qiSSa**

i جدّاً	
ii جّداً	**B -جدا**
iii جدّاً	very **giddan**

i شَقّة	
ii شُقّة	**C -شقة**
iii شقّة	apartment **shaqqa**

طَيّار i
طَيَار ii
طَيَار iii

D- طيـار
pilot **Tayyaar**

مّلك i
مَلكَ ii
مَلكِ iii

E- ملك
king **malik**

آسَف i
أسَف ii
آسِف iii

F- اسف
sorry **aasif**

سَيارة i
سَيّارة ii
سيّارة iii

G- سيارة
car **sayyaara**

H- شَعر
hair *sha^{c}r*

i شَعر	
ii شَعرَ	
iii شَعرِ	

I- شَعر
poetry *shi^{c}r*

i شَعرِ	
ii شَعرَ	
iii شَعرَ	

J- رجل
man *ragul*

i رَجل	
ii رَجُل	
iii رَجّل	

K- رجل
leg *rigl*

i رَجّل	
ii رَجّل	
iii رِجل	

96

Exercise 16

Vocalise the personal pronouns. Use the transliteration as your guide.

نحن -F
we **naHnu**

أنا-A
I **anaa**

أنتم -G
you (masculine, plural)
antum

أنت -B
you (masculine, singular)
anta

أنتن -H
you (feminine, plural)
antunna

أنت -C
you (feminine, singular)
anti

هم -I
they (masculine) **hum**

هو -D
he **huwa**

هن -ل
they (feminine) **hunna**

هي -E
she **hiya**

Exercise 17

Vocalise the Arabic verbs given below. Use the Arabic transliteration as your guide.

أكل -F

to eat *akala*

سمع -A

to hear *sami'a*

خرج -G

to exit *kharaga*

حب -B

to love *Habba*

شرب -H

to drink *shariba*

كتب -C

to write *kataba*

فتح -I

to open *fataHa*

نسي -D

to forget *nasiya*

ضحك -ل

to laugh *DaHika*

سأل -E

to ask *sa'ala*

Exercise 18

Can you vocalise the words given below? Use the English transliteration as a guide.

F- سمكة

fish **samaka**

A- رسام

painter **rassaam**

G- قمر

moon **qamar**

B- محطة

station **maHaTTa**

H- اقتصاد

economy **iqtisSaad**

C- فندق

hotel **funduk**

ا- قطار

train **qiTaar**

D- مشكلة

problem **mushkila**

ل- فعلا

indeed **fiᶜlan**

E- ستة

six **sitta**

99

Exercise 19

There is a four-letter word hidden in this puzzle. Can you find it?

Find and cross out each of the words listed on the facing page. Cross out the words vertically, horizontally, or diagonally. When you're done, you'll be left with the hidden word.

د	ر	س	ش	ج	د	م
م	ا	خ	ا	ل	ع	ح
ك	ر	ر	ر	ب	ب	ل
ا	ي	ح	ع	ن	ا	م
ت	ع	م	ب	ي	و	م
ب	ت	ح	ت	أ	ق	ف
ا	ه	ل	أ	ب	ح	ر

اهلاً
hello **ahlan**

ام
mother **umm**

اخ
brother **akh**

جد
grandfather **gadd**

تحت
underneath **taHt**

بحر
sea **baHr**

عم
uncle ͨ**amm**

شارع
street **shaari**ͨ

درس
lesson **dars**

لبن
milk **laban**

كاتب
writer **kaatib**

قف
stop **qif**

يوم
day **yawm**

محل
store **maHall**

مرحباً
welcome **marHaban**

Writing Exercises

Below are a number of exercises for you to practice
your writing. Remember to position the letter correctly
either above or underneath the line. Don't forget to place
the dots in their right places.

أستاذ   أستاذ   ـاذ

master/teacher ***ustaadh***

امرأة   امرأة   ـأة

woman ***imra'a***

برج   برج

tower ***burg***

بعيد   بعيد   ـيد

far ***ba͜eed***

102

توائم توائم
twins ***tawaa'im***

ثمن ثمن
price ***thaman***

جرس جرس
bell ***garas***

حارس حارس
guard ***Haaris***

حصان حصان
horse ***HiSaan***

103

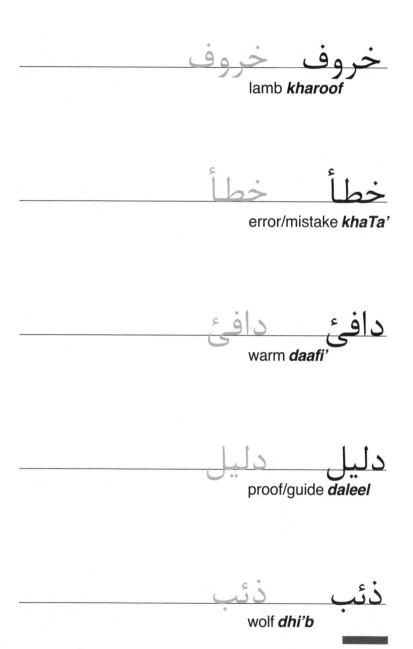

خروف   خروف
lamb *kharoof*

خطأ   خطأ
error/mistake *khaTa'*

دافئ   دافئ
warm *daafi'*

دليل   دليل
proof/guide *daleel*

ذئب   ذئب
wolf *dhi'b*

104

ریاح   رياح   رياح

wind *riyaaH*

زهرة   زهرة   زهرة

flower *zahra*

سيّارة   سيّارة   سيّارة

car *sayyaara*

شتاء   شتاء   شتاء

winter *shitaa'*

شرطة   شرطة   شرطة

police *shurTa*

105

صيدلية صيدلية

pharmacy **Saydaliya**

ضريبة ضريبة

tax **Dareeba**

ضيف ضيف

guest **Dayf**

طائرة طائرة

airplane **Taa'ira**

طبيب طبيب

doctor **Tabeeb**

106

ظلام   ظلام

darkness *Zalaam*

عروسة   عروسة

doll/bride *ᶜaroosa*

عنوان   عنوان

address *ᶜunwaan*

غرفة   غرفة

room *ghurfa*

غيور   غيور

jealous *ghayoor*

فائز   فائز

winner **faa'iz**

قلعة   قلعة

castle **qalᶜa**

قلب   قلب

heart **qalb**

كثير   كثير

much/many **katheer**

كوبري   كوبري

bridge **kubree**

108

لغة   لغة
language *lugha*

ليل   ليل
night *layl*

مدينة   مدينة
city *madeena*

مراهق   مراهق
teenager *muraahiq*

نجوم   نجوم
stars *nugoom*

هدوء　　هدوء
quietness *hudoo'*

هدية　　هدية
gift ***hadiya***

ولاء　　ولاء
loyalty ***walaa'***

يسار　　يسار
left ***yasaar***

يمين　　يمين
right **yameen**

واحد واحد
one **waaHid**

اثنان اثنان
two **ithnaan**

ثلاثة ثلاثة
three **thalaatha**

أربعة أربعة
four **arbaᶜa**

خمسة خمسة
five **khamsa**

ستة‎ سـتة

six *sitta*

سبعة‎ سـبعة

seven *sabᶜa*

ثمانية‎ ثمانية

eight *thamaaniya*

تسعة‎ تسعة

nine *tisᶜa*

عشرة‎ عشرة

ten *ᶜashara*

يوم يوم

day *yawm*

أسبوع أسبوع

week *usboo^c*

شهر شهر

month *shahr*

الأحد الأحد

Sunday *al-aHad*

الاثنين الاثنين

Monday *al-ithnayn*

113

الثلاثاء   الثلاثاء

Tuesday *al-thalaathaa'*

الأربعاء   الأربعاء

Wednesday *al-arbaᶜaa'*

الخميس   الخميس

Thursday *al-khamees*

الجمعة   الجمعة

Friday *al-gumᶜa*

السبت   السبت

Saturday *al-sabt*

اهلاً وسهلاً

hello & welcome ***ahlan wa-sahlan***

صباح الخير

good morning ***SabaaH al-khayr***

مساء الخير

good evening ***masaa' al-khayr***

السلام عليكم

peace be upon you (*a traditional greeting*)
as-salaamu ᶜalaykum

وعليكم السلام

and peace be upon you (*reply*)
wa-ᶜalaykum as-salaam

115

كيف حالك؟

how are you? *kayfa Haaluka?*

أنا بخير

I am fine *anaa bi-khayr*

كم الساعة؟

what is the time? *kam al-saaᶜa?*

العاشرة والربع

quarter past ten *al-ᶜaashira wa-al-rubᶜ*

شكراً

thank you *shukran*

116

من فضلك

please
min faDlaka

الحمدلّه

thank God
al-Hamdu lillaah

إن شاء اللّه

God willing
in shaa' allah

ما اسمك؟

what is your name?
maa ismuka

أنا اسمي ——

my name is ---
anaa ismee

117

ما عمرك؟

how old are you? *maa ᶜumruka?*

ماذا تعمل؟

what do you do? *maadha taᶜmal?*

أين تقيم؟

where do you live? *ayna tuqeem?*

من أين أنت؟

where are you from? *min ayna anta?*

هل تعرف العربية؟

do you know Arabic? *hal taᶜrif al-ᶜarabiya?*

118

أين الفندق؟

where is the hotel? *ayna al-funduq*

أريد خريطة

I want a map *ureedu khareeTa*

احتاج مساعدة

I need help *aHtaagu musaaᶜada*

مع السلامة

good bye *maᶜa as-salama*

إلى اللقاء

until we meet again *ilaa al-liqaa'*

119

Exercise 1

B-ق C-غ D-ك E-م F-ح G-ش H-ل I-ف J-ئ

Exercise 2

A-ک B-ض C-ث D-خ E-ظ F-س G-ي H-م I-ق J-ع

Exercise 3

B-نعم C-قلب D-صغير E-جبل F-صيف
G-ربيع H-شتاء I-خريف

Exercise 4

B-طريق C-سهم D-مغلق E-حرية F-صديق
G-خروج H-سلام I-مفتش

Exercise 5

B(i), C(v), D(ii), E(iv), F(vii), G(vi), H(xi), I(x), J(ix),
K (viii)

Exercise 6

Alphabetical order of Arab countries, reading from right to left:

الاردن- البحرين- المغرب- اليمن- تونس- سوريا-
قطر- لبنان- ليبيا- مصر

Exercise 7

Alphabetical order of Arab capitals, reading from right to left:

ابوظبي- الخرطوم- الرباط- الرياض- بغداد- بيروت-
دمشق-صنعاء- طرابلس- عمان

Exercise 8

A(v), B(iv), C(i), D(ii), E(iii)

Exercise 9

A(iv), B(v), C(iii), D(ii), E(i)

Exercise 10

٢ -E	٩٦ -D	٧٠ -C	٢٠٠ -B	٨٠ -A
٣٥ -J	٢٢ -I	٩٥ -H	٤ -G	٤٠ -F

Exercise 11

A(vi), B(iv), C(vii), D(i), E(ii), F(iii), G(v)

Exercise 12

A-بيت   B-سوق   C-سهم   D-نور   E-خطر

F-ممنوع G-جامعة H-صغير I-القاهرة J-أوتوبيس

K-جبل   L-حفلة   M-سكوت N-صحراء O-صديق

P-كلام   Q-عائلة   R-مغلق   S-مشكلة T-فاكهة

Exercise 13

A-يوم سعيد   B-البحر البعيد   C-جبل عالي

D-طفلة شقية   E-بيت قديم   F-المديرة الجديدة

G-حجرة نظيفة H-الدور الثاني

Exercise 14

B- المطعم الغالي   C- الرجل اللطيف   D- القهوة الساخنة

E- امرأة لطيفة   F- الشارع الضيق   G- الأخ الغني

H- الحجرة المغلقة   I- تذكرة رخيصة   J- العصير الطازج

F- الصديق الوفي

Exercise 15

C (i) شَقّة   B (iii) جِدّاً   A (iii) قصّة

F (iii) آسِف   E (iii) مَلِك   D (i) طَيّار

I (i) شِعر   H (i) شَعر   G (ii) سَيّارة

K (iii) رِجل   J (ii) رَجُل

Exercise 16

D- هُوَ   C- أنتِ   B- أنتَ   A - أَنَا

H- أنتُنَّ   G- أنتُم   F- نَحنُ   E- هِيَ

J - هُنَّ   I- هُم

122

Exercise 17

D- نَسِيَ	C- كَتَبَ	B- حَبَّ	A- سَمِعَ
H- شَرِبَ	G- خَرَجَ	F- أَكَلَ	E- سألَ
		ل- ضَحِكَ	ا- فَتَحَ

Exercise 18

D- مُشكِلة	C- فُندُق	B- مَحَطّة	A- رَسّام
H- إقتِصاد	G- قَمَر	F- سَمَكة	E- سِتّة
		ل- فِعلاً	ا- قِطار

Exercise 19

Missing word: عربي

Afterword

Congratulations, you have just learned the Arabic alphabet!

You have studied 28 letters, the hamza, vowel marks, numerals, and how to form the feminine. You have also been introduced to handwritten Arabic. By now, you should have a solid grasp of the Arabic script and feel confident enough to read and write basic words. You can now begin developing your vocabulary and learning basic grammatical structures. Remember, practice makes perfect, so continue by copying examples of Arabic writing you see in magazines, newspapers, books, etc.

Where will you go from here? It's up to you to decide!

It all depends on the degree of Arabic proficiency you want to achieve. You may want to continue with classical Arabic studies, learn the culture, learn to read and communicate, or just understand simple signs and instructions. You are now empowered with a strong basis of the Arabic script.

Good luck!

مع أطيب الأمنيات

The Arabic Alphabet

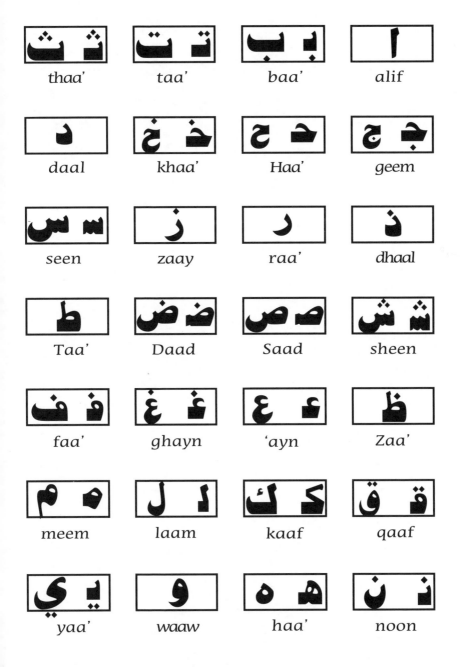

ثـ ثـ ث	تـ تـ ت	بـ بـ ب	ا
thaa'	taa'	baa'	alif
د	خـ خـ خ	حـ حـ ح	جـ جـ ج
daal	khaa'	Haa'	geem
سـ سـ س	ز	ر	ذ
seen	zaay	raa'	dhaal
ط	ضـ ضـ ض	صـ صـ ص	شـ شـ ش
Taa'	Daad	Saad	sheen
فـ فـ ف	غـ غـ غ	عـ عـ ع	ظ
faa'	ghayn	'ayn	Zaa'
مـ مـ م	لـ لـ لا	كـ كـ ك	قـ قـ ق
meem	laam	kaaf	qaaf
يـ يـ ي	و	هـ هـ ه	نـ نـ ن
yaa'	waaw	haa'	noon

Arabic is written from right to left, this workbook opens on the other side. It was designed this way to help you get used to the Arabic format of writing.

About the Author

Naglaa Ghali is a journalis͓   ...̇ʌrabic interpreter. She has devoted mucn of her own time to developing *funwitharabic.com*, an online program that uses a fun approach to learning Arabic. Ghali's approach helps learners of the Arabic language overcome the sometimes challenging and overwhelming intricacies of the Arabic script. In this new workbook, *Write it in Arabic,* Ghali extends that same principle to paper and provides students with hands-on experience in writing Arabic. Ghali is also the author of *Arabic Grammar Unravelled*, the ultimate guide to learning Modern Standard Arabic.

To learn more about Ghali and *Fun with Arabic,* visit her Web site at *www.funwitharabic.com.*